**This journal belongs to**

_____

**Date completed**

_____

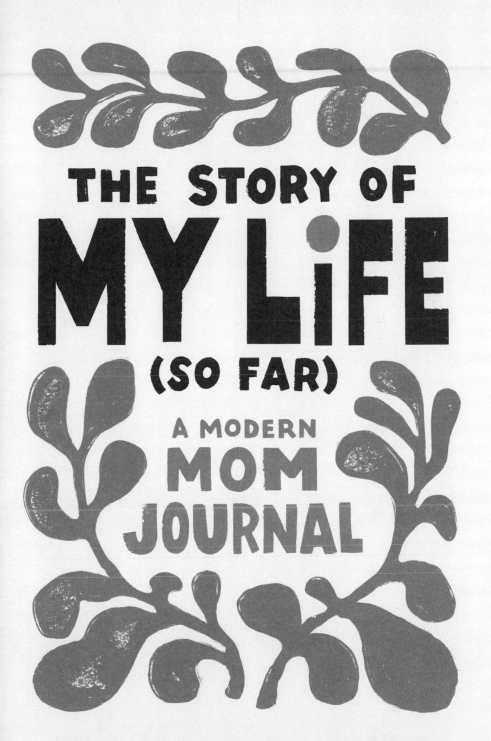

# THE STORY OF MY LIFE

## (SO FAR)

### A MODERN MOM JOURNAL

**TiFFANY DURRAH-BiLLINGSLEY**

ZEITGEIST • NEW YORK

To my three children: Makaela,
Parker Ellis, and Rhyan Kate.
You are my greatest gifts.

Published in the United States by Zeitgeist, an imprint of Zeitgeist™,
a division of Penguin Random House LLC, New York.
penguinrandomhouse.com

Zeitgeist™ is a trademark of Penguin Random House LLC

ISBN: 9780593436073

Hand lettering by Kelli Laderer
Author photo by Wendell Billingsley of Wen.He.Shoots Photography
Book design by Aimee Fleck

Printed in the United States of America

1 3 5 7 9 10 8 6 4 2

First Edition

# CONTENTS

THERE iS
MORE
HERE THAN
MEETS
THE EYE.
- MURASAKI SHiKiBU

# WRITING YOUR LIFE

*Hi!* I'm Tiffany Durrah-Billingsley, a corporate professional and a motherhood and lifestyle blogger. I am married to my husband, Wendell, and together we share three children, Makaela, Parker Ellis, and Rhyan Kate. I'm the youngest of three girls and was raised by my mother, a single parent, after the passing of my father when I was five years old. My mother relocated from Ohio to Alabama, where I grew up and attended college; I later moved to Texas, where I currently reside.

In 2020, after the birth of my youngest daughter, I experienced postpartum depression. I began journaling and found it to be very therapeutic, so much so that I created a blog (tiffanydurrah.com) as an outlet to share my personal motherhood journey. My content is centered on how to navigate life as a modern millennial woman. The goal: to encourage, inspire, and motivate women by sharing how to overcome the challenges life brings, find balance with it all, and never forget yourself along the way.

I remember having a conversation with my mom after going through postpartum depression where she revealed that she also endured a similar experience. It would have been wonderful if my mom had had a way to share her experience with me through writing. Now, with this journal, she can document these stories, and I can read all about her journey from a young girl to the woman she is today. I intend to do the same and pass down my story to my children, and I'm excited for you to do so as well.

As you go through this journal, I encourage you to authentically share of yourself, from your earliest memories up to the present. Our lives are unique—no two paths are exactly the same.

Think about how you have the opportunity to reflect on your personal journey so far, and even surprise yourself with the things you come up with. From you sharing your story, your children will gain a unique perspective of you as a mother and an individual, and will undoubtedly understand you (and perhaps even themselves) more deeply through the lens of your experience.

Motherhood is multifaceted, of course, and we are complex. We aren't just moms—we are so much more, and we each have a story worth sharing! This journal encompasses all aspects of life: our childhood, education, career, travel, philosophies, dreams, and overall life experiences. Our experiences shape our thoughts, beliefs, and ideals, and each experience continues to shape us as people. Today, you can begin filling in the blanks with all these experiences—the memories, stories, and inner workings that provide valuable insight into you as an individual.

The prompts throughout this journal are designed to help you reflect and allow you to capture your feelings about your past and present. As you prepare to write, try to find a quiet place for your reflections. This may not always be the easiest thing to do—after all, you're Mom!—but since reflection is an important part of self-care, take some time for yourself, grab your favorite pen, and wander through the pages until you find a prompt that sparks inspiration. You may discover that some questions don't apply to you; feel free to skip those prompts or tailor the questions to your specific circumstances.

There are no rules to journaling—you write as you're inspired, and that's what makes it beautiful. Enjoy journaling your life's experiences, and think about all the insights you can share with your children. This will be a wonderful keepsake!

A REAL MOM:
EMOTIONAL,
YET THE ROCK.
TIRED,
BUT KEEPS GOING.
WORRIED,
BUT FULL OF HOPE.
IMPATIENT,
YET PATIENT.
OVERWHELMED,
BUT NEVER QUITS.
AMAZING,
EVEN THOUGH DOUBTED.
WONDERFUL,
EVEN IN THE CHAOS.
LIFE CHANGER,
EVERY SINGLE DAY.
- RACHEL MARIE MARTIN

# CHAPTER 1

## *My Childhood*

Where were you born? What do you know about your birth? What stories do you know about the day you were brought into the world?

_____

_____

_____

_____

_____

_____

_____

_____

What were you like as a baby or toddler? How did your parent(s) or caregiver(s) describe you?

_____

_____

_____

_____

_____

_____

_____

_____

Describe how your parents met. How was their relationship? What favorite memory do you have of your parent(s) or caregiver(s) from childhood?

_____

_____

_____

_____

_____

_____

_____

_____

_____

_____

_____

In what ways did your parent(s) or caregiver(s) contribute to your upbringing? What do you model from their personalities? Their parenting styles?

_____

_____

_____

_____

_____

_____

_____

_____

_____

_____

_____

_____

Families come in many forms. They can be traditional, nontraditional, blended, made of people who care for us or those we choose for ourselves. Add your family members to the tree and show how they're linked.

Make a list of some of your parent(s)' or caregiver(s)' favorite songs. How do you feel when you hear them today? Which song is your favorite?

How did your parent(s) or caregiver(s) prepare you for bed or comfort you? What were your favorite bedtime or comforting moments? What made them special?

How many siblings do you have? How was your relationship during childhood? How did your birth order impact your relationship(s)?

Recall a time when you and your siblings competed. Who usually won? How did this impact the relationship you have now?

What were some of your favorite games or activities to play with your siblings? Did you ever play pranks on each other? What were they?

_____

_____

_____

_____

_____

_____

_____

_____

_____

_____

Name your grandparents. What is the earliest memory you have of each of your grandparents?

_____

_____

_____

_____

_____

_____

_____

_____

_____

_____

_____

_____

When you went to visit your grandparents or a favorite aunt, uncle, or family friend, what special things did you do? What memories did you create?

Which meals or dishes do you remember from your grandparents or another favorite person that you continue to make today? What are some memories or thoughts you have when you make them?

Recall the first time you started a new school or a first day of school. Growing up, what did you like most about school? What were some things you disliked?

_____

_____

_____

_____

_____

_____

_____

_____

_____

_____

_____

Describe how you felt about field trips. Where did you visit for a favorite trip? What made it memorable?

_____

_____

_____

_____

_____

_____

_____

_____

_____

_____

_____

_____

What kind of a student were you? What were your strengths? Weaknesses?

_____

_____

_____

_____

_____

_____

_____

_____

_____

Think about school lunch and recess. What is one of your strongest memories? Who did you sit with and play with?

_____

_____

_____

_____

_____

_____

_____

_____

_____

How did you meet your childhood best friend? If you can't remember, write about an early memory with them.

_____

_____

_____

_____

_____

_____

_____

_____

_____

_____

List some games and activities you enjoyed playing with your friends. Which were your favorite, and why? What is a funny memory?

_____

_____

_____

_____

_____

_____

_____

_____

_____

_____

_____

_____

Who was your childhood crush, whether a classmate or a celebrity? What did you like most about them, and why?

What secrets or rituals did you share with your friends?

Recall how you made new friends growing up. What did you find easy about making friends? What was difficult? Were you a social butterfly or more reserved?

_____

_____

_____

_____

_____

_____

_____

_____

_____

Describe the neighborhood where you grew up. What did the homes look like? Who were your neighbors? What places were nearby?

_____

_____

_____

_____

_____

_____

_____

_____

_____

_____

_____

Describe how you played with other children in your neighborhood. What are some memories you have of playing outside in your neighborhood?

_____

_____

_____

_____

_____

_____

_____

_____

_____

List the ways you explored your neighborhood. Who did you explore with? What were some of your favorite things to do, and why?

_____

_____

_____

_____

_____

_____

_____

_____

_____

_____

_____

_____

_____

List some events you had in your neighborhood. What were your favorites?

_____

_____

_____

_____

_____

_____

_____

_____

_____

_____

Who were some of your favorite neighbors? What made them special?
Were there any neighbors you didn't like? Why?

_____

_____

_____

_____

_____

_____

_____

_____

_____

_____

What did you have as a childhood pet? Who or what inspired your pet's name? How did you interact with your pet?

_____

_____

_____

_____

_____

_____

_____

_____

_____

List some of your favorite things you did with your pet. Share a favorite memory of your pet.

_____

_____

_____

_____

_____

_____

_____

_____

_____

_Fun Facts_

Did you collect anything as a child? If so, what?

What was your nickname growing up?

What were some of your favorite stores to visit?

How old were you when you learned Santa wasn't who you thought?

What was your favorite childhood TV show or movie?

Recall a time you got into trouble as a child. What happened? Did your actions have consequences? How did you feel?

_____

_____

_____

_____

_____

_____

_____

_____

_____

_____

What brought you comfort when you were scared, and why? If it was an item, how did you receive it? What eventually happened to it?

_____

_____

_____

_____

_____

_____

_____

_____

_____

_____

Describe how you spent Saturday mornings. What was a favorite cartoon or activity that you couldn't miss? What did you enjoy for breakfast?

Growing up, what chores were you responsible for? How were you rewarded for doing your chores?

List some of your favorite childhood dinners. What was your favorite meal growing up? Who prepared it? How often did you enjoy it?

_____

_____

_____

_____

_____

_____

_____

_____

_____

_____

_____

How did you learn right from wrong? Who were some people you looked up to?

_____

_____

_____

_____

_____

_____

_____

_____

_____

_____

_____

_____

_____

List ways you learned to express and give thanks. What was your favorite prayer, verse, or saying?

Describe ways you observed your spirituality. How did you gather with others? What is your favorite memory of a religious, spiritual, or feel-good celebration?

List some holiday traditions you and your family enjoyed. Which was your favorite, and why? What did you do during that time together? What foods did you like?

_____

_____

_____

_____

_____

_____

_____

_____

_____

_____

Describe a time during childhood when you stayed up late to count down to midnight on New Year's Eve. How did you and your family celebrate the new year?

_____

_____

_____

_____

_____

_____

_____

_____

_____

_____

What is one of your fondest summer memories with family, at home or away?

How did you celebrate your birthdays? Which celebration was most memorable, and why?

## Lessons Learned

What was a mistake that you made in your childhood? How did you learn from your mistakes?

IT'S ABOUT
A GIRL
WHO IS ON THE
CUSP OF BECOMING
SOMEONE...
A GIRL WHO MAY
NOT KNOW WHAT
SHE WANTS RIGHT
NOW, AND SHE
MAY NOT KNOW WHO
SHE IS RIGHT NOW,
BUT WHO DESERVES
THE CHANCE TO
FIND OUT.
- JODI PICOULT

## CHAPTER 2

# Growing Up to Be Me

What were your favorite books, shows, and/or movies as a teen?

_____

_____

_____

_____

_____

_____

_____

_____

_____

What memories do you have of becoming a teenager? What were you most excited about? What was something you dreaded?

_____

_____

_____

_____

_____

_____

_____

_____

_____

How was your attitude toward your family during your teen years? How did the relationship with your family members change?

_____

_____

_____

_____

_____

_____

_____

_____

_____

_____

_____

Describe a time when you got into trouble. Did you regret it? If so, what things did you say or do that you wish you hadn't?

_____

_____

_____

_____

_____

_____

_____

_____

_____

_____

_____

_____

How did your parent(s) or caregiver(s) help you navigate adolescence? What was one of the toughest things you had to deal with or overcome?

Recall a time you disagreed with your parent(s)' or caregiver(s)' decision. Looking back on it, how do you feel about it now?

When you were growing up, how did your family create new memories together? What is one of your fondest memories, and why?

_____
_____
_____
_____
_____
_____
_____
_____
_____
_____

Did your family vacation? If so, where? How did you travel? What was one of your favorite places to visit? If you didn't vacation, how about day trips?

_____
_____
_____
_____
_____
_____
_____
_____
_____
_____
_____
_____
_____
_____

How did you and your family communicate about what happened during the day? How did you spend one-on-one time?

_____

_____

_____

_____

_____

_____

_____

_____

What was the first school dance you attended? Describe a funny or embarrassing moment. What happened? Who was involved?

_____

_____

_____

_____

_____

_____

_____

_____

_____

*Fun Facts*

As a teen, would you rather have washed dishes, mowed the lawn, or folded the laundry?

If you could have joined a music group, which one would it have been, and why?

What's one thing you would never do again?

What was your favorite fashion trend?

What was the craziest thing you did as a dare?

What activities did you participate in during your school years? What are some of your best memories of them?

_____
_____
_____
_____
_____
_____
_____
_____
_____
_____

What is one accomplishment that you're most proud of? How did your family react?

_____
_____
_____
_____
_____
_____
_____
_____
_____
_____

What significant event do you recall about freshman year? How did high school change for you throughout the years?

Describe a teacher or administrator who was influential in your life. Who were they? In what ways did they inspire you?

How did you feel about attending prom? Describe your prom. What did you wear? Who did you go with? What made it special, not so special, or otherwise notable?

_____

_____

_____

_____

_____

_____

_____

_____

_____

Describe your favorite school event. What made it memorable? What was the most exciting thing about the event?

_____

_____

_____

_____

_____

_____

_____

_____

_____

_____

_____

# ALL ABOUT ME
## (IN HIGH SCHOOL)

**NAME**

**ADDRESS**

**MY FRiENDS**

**CLUBS
(& OTHER
ACTiViTiES)**

**MY FAVORiTE**

**CLASS**

**TEACHER**

**SONG**

**SPORTS**

Describe your high school graduation day. What made your graduation memorable? How did you feel?

_____

_____

_____

_____

_____

_____

_____

_____

_____

_____

Who was your best friend during high school? How did you meet them? How did the relationship change during your teen years?

_____

_____

_____

_____

_____

_____

_____

_____

_____

_____

_____

Describe an argument you had with a friend. How did you and your friend settle the dispute? How did it change the relationship, if at all?

Make a list of your friends from your teenage years. Who are you still friends with? How often do you communicate?

Describe going on your first date. Who were you with? Where did you go? What did you do?

_____

_____

_____

_____

_____

_____

_____

_____

_____

_____

Recall your first kiss. How old were you? Who was it with? How did it make you feel? Who did you share the details about the moment with?

_____

_____

_____

_____

_____

_____

_____

_____

_____

_____

_____

_____

Think about the first time you fell in love. Who was it? Who said "I love you" first? How did you know? How did it make you feel?

Describe your first breakup. How did you feel, and how did you deal with your emotions? Who was there to help you?

Describe your first job. Where did you work? What are some of your favorite memories? What did you learn and how did it prepare you for the future?

_____

_____

_____

_____

_____

_____

_____

_____

_____

_____

_____

Make a list of paid jobs or volunteer experiences you had before adulthood. What skills did you learn?

_____

_____

_____

_____

_____

_____

_____

_____

_____

_____

_____

_____

What did you enjoy doing during the summer as a teen? Who did you spend your summers with?

_____

_____

_____

_____

_____

_____

_____

_____

_____

_____

Describe your favorite hangout spot as a teen. Who did you spend time with? What were some things you enjoyed doing?

_____

_____

_____

_____

_____

_____

_____

_____

_____

_____

_____

Describe something that changed in the world when you were a teen. Where were you when it happened? How did you find out?

_____

_____

_____

_____

_____

_____

_____

_____

_____

_____

Do you recall turning 16? How did you celebrate the milestone? What made it memorable?

_____

_____

_____

_____

_____

_____

_____

_____

_____

_____

What was the first or best concert you attended? Who performed? Who did you go with? Did anything exciting happen?

_____

_____

_____

_____

_____

_____

_____

_____

_____

How did you learn to drive? Who helped teach you? What fears did you have about driving?

_____

_____

_____

_____

_____

_____

_____

_____

_____

_____

Were you a responsible driver? Explain why or why not. How old were you when you got your first ticket?

_____

_____

_____

_____

_____

_____

_____

_____

_____

_____

Describe your first car. What make and model was it? What was your favorite thing about it?

_____

_____

_____

_____

_____

_____

_____

_____

_____

_____

Think about your first voting experience. Who was running for office? How did you feel participating in the election?

_____

_____

_____

_____

_____

_____

_____

_____

_____

What did you decide to do after high school? Who or what influenced your decision?

_____

_____

_____

_____

_____

_____

_____

_____

_____

_____

*Fun Facts*

What was your favorite song? Favorite singer?

Did you ever hit anything while driving? What did you hit?

Did you ever have a secret admirer? Who was it?

Did you ever cheat on a test?

Did you ever sneak out of the house? Did you get caught?

After high school, what were your thoughts about moving out of your childhood home? How did staying close to family or the desire to relocate influence you?

What goals did you set for yourself after high school? What steps did you take to accomplish them? What unexpected things happened along the way?

What was your idea of a dream job? How did your ideas change? How did they stay the same?

_____

_____

_____

_____

_____

_____

Describe your thoughts of starting a family. What were your ideas about marriage and children?

_____

_____

_____

_____

_____

_____

# Lessons Learned

Looking back on your teen years, what was the most valuable thing you learned? What would you tell your own teen about this lesson?

FOR ME, **BECOMING**
ISN'T ABOUT
ARRIVING SOMEWHERE
OR ACHIEVING
A CERTAIN AIM.
**I SEE IT INSTEAD AS**
A FORWARD MOTION,
A MEANS OF EVOLVING
AND A WAY TO REACH
CONTINUOUSLY TOWARD
A BETTER SELF.
THE JOURNEY
DOESN'T END.
— MICHELLE OBAMA

# CHAPTER 3

# Coming Into My Own

Describe the steps you took after high school. Did you attend college or additional school, or enter the military or the workforce? How did you feel about this?

_____

_____

_____

_____

_____

_____

_____

_____

How did you adjust to being responsible for your own schedule? What did you find most challenging?

_____

_____

_____

_____

_____

_____

_____

_____

How did your family dynamic change as you reached adulthood? What remained the same?

_____

_____

_____

_____

_____

_____

_____

_____

_____

_____

_____

Describe leaving your family for the first time. Where did you go? How did you feel?

_____

_____

_____

_____

_____

_____

_____

_____

_____

_____

_____

How did the bond between you and your parent(s) or caregiver(s) change as you entered adulthood? How did it stay the same?

Describe how your perspective of your parent(s) or caregiver(s) changed during adulthood. What things did you learn about them?

How did you process your emotions of losing a family member? What memories do you cherish of them?

Describe how you found support in family members during difficult times. Who did you lean on for guidance?

Did you have a balance between work and fun?
What steps did you take to make sure both
happened? What was your philosophy?

_____

_____

_____

_____

_____

_____

_____

_____

_____

Recount your first move after leaving your
childhood home. Did you live alone or with
someone else? How did you feel about your
new home?

_____

_____

_____

_____

_____

_____

_____

*Fun Facts*

If you could have done
anything after high school,
what would it have been?

How long was your most
recent relationship
before your current one?

What family member do
you particularly connect
with?

What was the longest
road trip you took after
high school?

What was a vice you
had? Do you still have it?

Describe the neighborhood where you found your first home. What were some things that you loved about it?

_____

_____

_____

_____

_____

_____

_____

_____

_____

_____

Do you have any keepsakes from your first home?

_____

_____

_____

_____

_____

_____

_____

_____

_____

_____

_____

_____

What are some things you received as gifts for your first home? Which items do you have today?

What memories, celebrations, and milestones did you have in your first home?

Describe your fondest memory of your first home. What made it special?

_____

_____

_____

_____

_____

_____

_____

_____

_____

_____

How did you feel after leaving your first home? What prompted the transition?

_____

_____

_____

_____

_____

_____

_____

_____

_____

_____

_____

Describe your first job interview as an adult. What was the outcome? How did you feel?

_____

_____

_____

_____

_____

_____

_____

_____

_____

_____

Recall the first job offer you received as an adult. What was the job description?

_____

_____

_____

_____

_____

_____

_____

_____

_____

_____

How have you cultivated meaningful relationships with your coworkers?
How did the relationships grow? How do you interact with colleagues?

Who gave you career advice or mentored you? How did it benefit your
career?

Describe a time when you experienced conflict in the workplace. How did you handle it?

_____

_____

_____

_____

_____

_____

_____

_____

_____

_____

Recall a time when you received a promotion or accolades at work. What steps did you take to achieve it?

_____

_____

_____

_____

_____

_____

_____

_____

_____

_____

_____

Describe a time you had to leave a job. What happened? If it was your choice, what were some factors in your decision?

_____

_____

_____

_____

_____

_____

_____

_____

_____

_____

Recall when you traveled to a favorite place. Where did you go? What exciting things happened?

_____

_____

_____

_____

_____

_____

_____

_____

_____

_____

_____

How often do you travel? What methods of transportation do you take? Which method do you prefer?

Describe a time when something unexpected happened while traveling. What was it? How did you handle the situation?

Make a list of all the places you've visited. Which is your favorite, and why?

_____

_____

_____

_____

_____

_____

_____

_____

_____

Describe a time you met someone while traveling. Where did you meet?
Who initiated the conversation?

_____

_____

_____

_____

_____

_____

_____

_____

_____

_____

_____

List some things you love to do when traveling.

When deciding to go on a trip, how do you plan? How are you spontaneous? Which is your preference—well-planned or spur-of-the-moment? Why?

Describe your budget strategy to maintain your first household. Who was responsible for managing the household? How did you come to this decision?

_____

_____

_____

_____

_____

_____

_____

_____

_____

_____

_____

_____

What are some things you wish you'd known about budgeting in your early adulthood?

_____

_____

_____

_____

_____

_____

_____

_____

_____

_____

_____

_____

How do you decide what's for dinner during the week? How often do you cook at home, take out, or eat out at a restaurant?

How did you adjust to living on your own? How did you entertain yourself at home when you were alone? What were some things you enjoyed?

Describe a house party you went to. What was the occasion? Do you prefer to be the hostess or guest? Why?

_____

_____

_____

_____

_____

_____

_____

_____

_____

_____

_____

How did you adjust to living with someone else? How do you share responsibilities? What do you find easy? What is difficult?

_____

_____

_____

_____

_____

_____

_____

_____

_____

_____

_____

What did a typical day look like in your
twenties? How much time did you spend
on work, leisure, social activities, and so on?
Divide up your day on this 24-hour clock.

12 AM

9 PM

3 AM

6 AM

3 PM

9 AM

12 PM

Describe how you managed relationships during early adulthood. What challenges did you face?

_____

_____

_____

_____

_____

_____

_____

_____

_____

_____

Make a list of some new friends you made as an adult. Who are you still friends with? How often do you connect with them?

_____

_____

_____

_____

_____

_____

_____

_____

_____

_____

_____

What was the worst argument you had with a partner? What happened? Who was first to apologize, if anyone? How did you resolve the conflict?

Describe the relationship you had with your best friend in your early adult years. How did you meet? What made the relationship special?

Describe how your friendships changed as an adult. Do you find it harder or easier to make new friends? Why?

_____

_____

_____

_____

_____

_____

_____

_____

_____

_____

Explain how dating during adulthood changed. How did your views and expectations change?

_____

_____

_____

_____

_____

_____

_____

_____

_____

_____

_____

_____

What was the worst breakup you experienced? Who initiated it, and why? Looking back, what did you learn from the experience?

Do you consider yourself a leader or a follower? Why?

What day of the week is your favorite, and why? How do you like spending that day?

_____

_____

_____

_____

_____

_____

_____

_____

_____

_____

_____

What was most important to you as a young adult, and how has it changed?

_____

_____

_____

_____

_____

_____

_____

_____

_____

_____

_____

_____

How confident were you as a young adult, and how has that changed?

Looking back on your young adult self, how would you describe her?

If you had a live-in partner or spouse as a young adult that you don't have now, what happened?

_____

_____

_____

_____

_____

_____

_____

_____

_____

What lessons did that relationship teach you?

_____

_____

_____

_____

_____

_____

_____

_____

_____

_____

What's one thing you wish you knew prior to adulthood? What would you share with your younger self? Why is this advice so important?

_____

_____

_____

_____

_____

_____

_____

_____

_____

_____

_____

What was the most embarrassing thing that happened to you as an adult so far?

_____

_____

_____

_____

_____

_____

_____

_____

_____

_____

_____

_____

Recall a time when you laughed hysterically. What were you doing? Were you alone? Did you share this experience with others?

_____

_____

_____

_____

_____

_____

_____

_____

_____

_____

What moment in time did you feel was a once-in-a-lifetime experience? What made it so memorable? Who was involved?

_____

_____

_____

_____

_____

_____

_____

_____

_____

_____

_____

_____

Recall a time when you tried something new. What was it? How did it feel to step out of your comfort zone? Any regrets?

_____

_____

_____

_____

_____

_____

_____

_____

_____

_____

_____

How did you meet your current partner? Who made the first move? How long have you been together?

_____

_____

_____

_____

_____

_____

_____

_____

_____

_____

_____

_____

What are your relationship goals? Who are some of your best role models? What steps can you take to reach your goals?

_____

_____

_____

_____

_____

_____

_____

_____

_____

_____

_____

_____

_____

Describe your first date with your current partner. What first attracted you to them? List the characteristics you've loved about them, both then and now.

_____

_____

_____

_____

_____

_____

_____

_____

_____

_____

_____

_____

Describe your relationship with your partner. What things do you want to stay the same? What things would you like to change?

What is your viewpoint on marriage? How have your views changed? How have they stayed the same?

If married, what did you wear on your wedding day? Who was there? What was the best thing about the day?

_____

_____

_____

_____

_____

_____

_____

_____

_____

Describe your relationship with your in-laws. What are some of the things you value about them?

_____

_____

_____

_____

_____

_____

_____

_____

_____

_____

The Story of My Life (So Far)

Describe the relationship between your in-laws and your children.

_____

_____

_____

_____

_____

_____

_____

_____

_____

_____

When did you feel like a true adult? Was there a specific moment you realized it, or was it a gradual process?

_____

_____

_____

_____

_____

_____

_____

_____

*Fun Facts*

Which family member knows you best?

Which family member knows you the least?

What is the best gift you have given someone?

What is the worst gift you have ever received?

How many times have you been married?

Describe your spiritual views. Do you have the same spiritual beliefs from your childhood? How did your views change after becoming an adult? What prompted the change?

When times are tough, how do you find strength? Do you rely on your spiritual beliefs for support? Share the ways you seek strength.

Make a list of things you're grateful for. In what ways do you like to express gratitude? How often do you express it?

_____

_____

_____

_____

_____

_____

_____

What's something difficult that's happened to you that resulted in a positive lesson learned? What was the lesson?

_____

_____

_____

_____

_____

_____

## Lessons Learned

What was something your parent(s) or caregiver(s) did or didn't do that you want to do differently?

# CHAPTER 4
## The Mom Years

How did you feel when you first became a mother? What advice would you give your younger self to help prepare for motherhood?

_____

_____

_____

_____

_____

_____

_____

_____

_____

Describe how you created your family. How did you come to the decision of how many children to have? Did you and your partner agree?

_____

_____

_____

_____

_____

_____

_____

_____

Think about the experience you had creating your family. How was the process? Was it easier or harder than expected? How?

_____

_____

_____

_____

_____

_____

_____

_____

_____

_____

Describe your child/children's birth story. Relate the plan you set. How was the reality the same or different? What are some things you wished you'd known?

_____

_____

_____

_____

_____

_____

_____

_____

_____

_____

_____

List some mothers whose parenting style you admire. What do you admire about them, and how have they influenced your parenting style?

Describe the most embarrassing thing that has happened to you in public during motherhood. Where were you? Who witnessed it?

Describe your mother or caregiver's parenting style. What did you gain from their parenting style that you have implemented in your own?

Explain the way you decided to feed your baby. Describe the journey. Was there anything you liked, didn't like, or wish you'd done differently?

Describe your parenting style. How do you and your partner's styles differ?
How are they the same? How do you compromise?

What do you want your child/children to remember about their childhood?

If you could share one thing with your child/children, what would it be? What lessons do you hope they carry with them through life?

_____

_____

_____

_____

_____

_____

_____

_____

_____

_____

Revisit the first time you left your child/children with a babysitter or at daycare. How did you feel?

_____

_____

_____

_____

_____

_____

_____

_____

_____

_____

_____

_____

Describe your child/children's first school experience. How did they adjust to their first day? What emotions did you feel?

_____

_____

_____

_____

_____

_____

_____

_____

_____

How did you come to the decision to no longer expand your family? How did you cope with the decision?

_____

_____

_____

_____

_____

_____

_____

_____

How did you make the decision to stay home or to work outside of the home or remotely? What influenced the decision? Would you change anything?

Describe the first time you returned to work after expanding your family. How long did it take you to return? How did you feel?

Describe your job. What steps do you take to find balance in your career and motherhood? If you travel for work, how does this feel?

If you are a stay-at-home mom, describe your feelings on this. What benefits do you enjoy most? What do you miss?

There's a saying "There's no such thing as a nonworking mother." Do you feel supported and appreciated in your role? Explain why or why not.

Was there ever a time you missed an event or moment in your child/children's life because of work commitments? How did you process your feelings?

List goals you have for your career. What steps are you taking or hoping to take to achieve these goals? How will you overcome challenges?

Was there ever a time you had to turn down a job or assignment because of family commitments? Is there anything you would do differently if you could do it over?

How do you balance work and life? What helps or hinders your focus?

Do you find joy in your current position? What would you like to do differently?

Recall the first time you traveled without your children. Who were you with? How did you feel? How did you process your emotions?

Describe your dream vacation. Where would you like to visit? Who would go? Would it be a family, girls', couples', or solo trip?

Describe your favorite vacation with your child/children. Where did you go? What made it fun? Did anything exciting or memorable happen?

_____

_____

_____

_____

_____

_____

_____

_____

_____

_____

_____

What kind of travelers are your child/children? How do you prepare for travel with them? What tricks have you learned along the way?

_____

_____

_____

_____

_____

_____

_____

_____

_____

_____

_____

As a mom, what are your favorite things to do with your child/children while traveling? What feels special about these times?

Think back to your first family vacation. Where did you go? What memorable things happened? What new memories did you create?

Describe the funniest or most embarrassing thing that happened during a family trip. How did you deal with it?

_____

_____

_____

_____

_____

_____

_____

_____

_____

_____

In a perfect world, how often would you travel? Where is someplace new you'd like to go?

_____

_____

_____

_____

_____

_____

_____

_____

_____

_____

How important is seeing new places to you? What are you most drawn to? Is it culture, relaxation, cuisine, history, or something else, and why?

How did you meet your first mom friend? How did the relationship develop?

# PLACES I'VE LIVED

# PLACES I'VE VISITED

What efforts do you make to connect with other moms? Are you shy or outgoing? Social or reserved? What activities do you enjoy doing with other moms?

_____

_____

_____

_____

_____

_____

_____

_____

_____

_____

Describe a situation where you needed advice from a friend. How have you found support with your friends? Are you more likely to give or take advice?

_____

_____

_____

_____

_____

_____

_____

_____

_____

_____

How do you foster relationships with friends since becoming a mom? How do you show yourself to be friendly? How do you think others see you?

List some friends you have made since becoming a mom. How have friendships been beneficial to you during your motherhood journey?

What is the best thing your partner has said to you or about you since becoming parents?

_____

_____

_____

_____

_____

_____

_____

_____

_____

_____

_____

Describe your and your partner's philosophies on relationships. Which ideas do you agree on? Which do you disagree on?

_____

_____

_____

_____

_____

_____

_____

_____

_____

_____

_____

_____

Describe your and your partner's philosophies on parenting. Which beliefs do you agree on? Which do you disagree on?

What fun things do you do as a couple since becoming parents that you never did before?

What about parenting makes your partnership stronger? What has tested it?

How has parenting changed you as a partner? How has parenting changed your partner?

Which family members have you grown closer to as a result of parenting? Why and how?

_____

_____

_____

_____

_____

_____

_____

_____

_____

Which family members do you see making an impact on your child/children and in what ways?

_____

_____

_____

_____

_____

_____

_____

_____

_____

_____

_____

How many pairs of shoes do you own?

Do you prefer coffee or tea? How do you take it?

What's the longest amount of time you have gone without sleep? Why?

Are you a clean or messy person?

Who is your favorite author, and why?

Make a list of some new traditions you've started with your family. How did you come up with these ideas?

_____

_____

_____

_____

_____

_____

_____

_____

_____

_____

What are some traditions that were passed down from your childhood or your partner's that you continue with your family?

_____

_____

_____

_____

_____

_____

_____

_____

_____

_____

_____

List some ways you celebrate with your child/children. How do you document the moments? What are some things you want them to remember?

What are some traditions that you have started with your family to celebrate the holidays? Which holiday tradition is your favorite?

What do you hope your child/children take with them from the celebrations and traditions you've established?

_____

_____

_____

_____

_____

_____

_____

_____

_____

_____

As your child/children grow, what milestones mean the most, and why? What milestones do you look forward to?

_____

_____

_____

_____

_____

_____

_____

_____

_____

_____

_____

_____

Describe a family tradition or ritual that has a special meaning. What makes it special? Who is involved?

_____

_____

_____

_____

_____

_____

_____

_____

_____

_____

Why is it important for your family to make new traditions? Why is it important to keep old ones?

_____

_____

_____

_____

_____

_____

_____

_____

_____

_____

_____

Describe your typical day. How do you get everything done? What task(s) do you wish you could delegate?

_____

_____

_____

_____

_____

_____

_____

_____

_____

_____

How are you planning for your family's future? What hopes do you have for your family?

_____

_____

_____

_____

_____

_____

_____

_____

_____

_____

_____

Explore your idea of a balanced lifestyle. What do you do to find balance in motherhood? What would you like to do differently?

Make a list of your stressors. List your favorite ways to relieve stress.

What are your favorite self-care activities, and why?

What's your favorite "rabbit-hole" activity that gets you off course from your day?

List the ways you make time for yourself. How do you spend quiet time?

What's your favorite music? What do you listen to in the car: music, news, podcasts, or audiobooks? Or do you prefer silence?

Who is a public figure you admire, and why?

How do you feel about the pets you have or don't have? Do you wish you had some, and if so, what kind?

List your household responsibilities. Describe how you and your partner share responsibilities. How did you come to this decision?

Was there anything about motherhood that surprised you?

Describe a time you sought advice from someone to help you navigate a problem. What was it? How did they help you?

_____

_____

_____

_____

_____

_____

What would you like your kids to know about you?

_____

_____

_____

_____

_____

_____

## *Lessons Learned*

What has motherhood taught you? How has your motherhood journey given you a greater appreciation for your own mother or caregiver(s)?

Hi there,

We hope you enjoyed using *The Story of My Life (So Far)*. If you have any questions or concerns about your book, or have received a damaged copy, please contact **customerservice@penguinrandomhouse.com**. We're here and happy to help.

Also, please consider writing a review on your favorite retailer's website to let others know what you thought of the book!

Sincerely,

*The Zeitgeist Team*